PLANET HERO!

365 Ways to Save the Earth

Lauren Wechsler Horn

STERLING INNOVATION
An imprint of Sterling Publishing Co., Inc.

New York / London
www.sterlingpublishing.com/kids

STERLING, the Sterling logo, STERLING INNOVATION, and the Sterling Innovation logo
are registered trademarks of Sterling Publishing Co., Inc.

Library of Congress Cataloging-in-Publication Data Available

10 9 8 7 6 5 4 3 2 1

Published by Sterling Publishing Co., Inc.
387 Park Avenue South, New York, NY 10016

© 2009 by Lauren Wechsler Horn

Distributed in Canada by Sterling Publishing
c/o Canadian Manda Group, 165 Dufferin Street
Toronto, Ontario, Canada M6K 3H6
Distributed in the United Kingdom by GMC Distribution Services
Castle Place, 166 High Street, Lewes, East Sussex, England BN7 1XU
Distributed in Australia by Capricorn Link (Australia) Pty. Ltd.
P.O. Box 704, Windsor, NSW 2756, Australia

Illustrations by Beth Mueller

Printed in China
Sterling ISBN 978-1-4027-6281-9

For information about custom editions, special sales, premium and
corporate purchases, please contact Sterling Special Sales
Department at 800-805-5489 or specialsales@sterlingpublishing.com

DEDICATION

The world was not left to us by our parents, it was lent to us by our children.
African Proverb

Unless someone like you cares a whole awful lot, nothing is going to get better. It's not.
The Lorax by Dr. Seuss

This book is dedicated to Ella Harris and Joss Harper, both of whom are growing up to be extraordinary guardians of our planet. I love you with all my heart.

ACKNOWLEDGMENTS

There were so many cooks that made this book possible. First and foremost I would like to thank my sister-in-law, Pamela Horn, whose trust, faith, and vision enabled me to take part in this transformational and inspirational project. Thank you to Cindy Katz, my editor, who kept me on track and (mostly) on deadline. To the Ethical Culture Fieldston School in New York City, which is an educational leader in environmental practices—from installing a Green Dean to developing rooftop gardens and obtaining LEED certification. Also at the same school, a huge thank you to all the wonderful Fieldston Lower parents and students who contributed their thoughtful comments and suggestions, including this gem from a pre-K student, "families who are *really* close should reuse toilet paper to save trees." A big nod of admiration to Sandy Diaz, Suzanne Hockstein, and Susan Smelin from the Riverdale Nursery School and Family Center, one of the first, and possibly only, green preschools in the country. Their creative and progressive curriculum has shown many a naysayer that even two-year-olds can be taught to recycle. I thank Dan Oko for his many interesting points-of-view and wealth of resources. Our conversations helped me to focus and organize my thoughts. To Ella and Joss, I give a big hug of thanks for their patience, love, and understanding, especially when they would ask how I was helping the planet when I was on the computer so much. Finally, to my wonderful husband Peter, whose love, support, humor, and deep understanding got me through some late nights and even earlier mornings. Thank you for indulging my work hours and my zaniness.

CONTENTS

· ·

• •

INTRODUCTION

These days it's easy to get caught up in the doom-and-gloom scenarios of not taking care of our planet. This book is intended as a solution. There are many actions you can take to make a real and sustainable difference (see the "Key Terms" list on page 13 to learn the background on sustainability and other important topics discussed throughout these pages). You don't have to turn your life upside down or make your parents, teachers, and friends crazy to make a lasting change. Try not to go nuts and get lost in the little details, but rather sit back and challenge yourself to think differently about how you look at and interact with our world.

Reducing global warming and saving the planet are pretty big and complex tasks for even the smartest adults and governments. So don't get frustrated and think you can't help make a better, cleaner, and healthier planet. Know that even your small actions can make a big difference. The good thing about the environmental problems we face is that there are so many points of intervention. That means that there are lots and lots of places to plug in, to get involved, and to make a noticeable change. Contrary to what many commercials on TV tell you to purchase, there is no single simple thing to do or to buy, because the set of problems we're addressing just isn't simple.

It's important that you address both the big-picture stuff and your day-to-day personal impacts and lifestyle changes. Moving toward greater sustainability and zero waste is necessary, but truly believing and understanding that supporting a green way of life should not be reduced to consumer choices is what you should always remember. Shopping is not the solution to the environmental problems we currently face because the real changes we need just aren't for sale in even the most eco-friendly and greenest stores. Of course, when you and your family do shop for necessities, you should ensure your dollars support businesses that protect the environment and worker rights. But educate yourself and train those around you to look beyond unclear claims on packages to find the hard facts. Despite your desire to run out and buy a new hemp and organic cotton wardrobe, buying less is really the best option of all. If we collectively buy less, we decrease pollution and decrease waste and landfills. Isn't this one of the biggest and simplest things we can all do to help our planet?

In addition to personal waste reduction and the promotion of sustainability, young people like you must support and pursue environmental justice at multiple levels. True planetary sustainability means that pollution-free air, clean water, healthy food, and safe consumer choices are available to all people in your community and the world, not just those that can afford to live in a toxic-free area or to visit an upscale organic produce market.

In the WATER, LAND, and ANIMALS sections of the book you'll learn valuable tips to reduce consumption (what you typically buy and acquire on a daily basis) and waste while also learning to promote less toxic alternatives to everyday activities. In these sections you can see how reconnecting with nature helps you get back in touch with the planet. You are part of nature so act as though you are. Understand your place in the world and how you affect it and how it affects you.

In the ENERGY section you will learn how to reduce the energy used by your family and in your home. Valuable tips will help change your behavior to become less energy dependent and to reduce your carbon footprint. By the way, you'll be reading a lot about carbon footprints in this book, so let me explain. A carbon footprint is a measure of the impact that your actions have on the environment in terms of the amount of greenhouse gases produced by your activity. It is measured in units of carbon dioxide emitted and is meant to be useful to understand your personal impact in contributing to global warming. Essentially it means that it is possible to calculate how much or how little damage you are doing through your everyday activities like using a computer, taking a shower, or riding in a car. It's fun and easy to find carbon footprint calculators on the Internet, but make sure your parents or another trusted adult knows you're conducting online research.

The REDUCE, REUSE, RECYCLE section is all about consumption. It will teach you that the three primary "R"s are the first step toward solving our garbage and trash problem. If we think about what kinds of things we can reuse, repair, or recycle before we buy them, we won't purchase as many things that will eventually turn into waste. Two other good "R"s to remember are repair and respect. In combination, the five "R"s not only reduce our waste disposal problems, but they also keep us from depleting our natural resources.

In this context consumption not only means what you buy, collect, and save every day, but it also means paying closer attention to what you currently own and what you *really* need to live on. Try comparing your true living "needs" to your "wants." A new pair of sneakers because you outgrew your old ones (need) vs. your 15th pair of jeans (want). You will most likely see that you require fewer resources than you originally thought you really needed.

HEALTH and FOOD provides tips to encourage you to eat simply and buy locally. It also gives health advice that will improve both the shape of your body and the shape of our environment.

The SEASONS and HOLIDAYS, CELEBRATIONS, and BIRTHDAYS sections provide creative tips on environmentally-conscious homemade and consumer choices (if you have to give a gift, it might as well be green, right?).

AWARENESS and ACTION focuses on consciousness-raising activities that you need to know in order to successfully change the attitudes and actions of those around you.

The WOW FACTS! throughout give staggering statistics that should get your attention and really make you think. The ART PROJECTS are just plain fun—some of them require help from your parents which is a great way to get them involved in the green movement! After a long, hard day of school and trying to save the world, remember that you're still young and that your parents were once young too. Grab their hands, show them the directions in the book, and ask them to help you with the activities.

Lastly, remember that this book is meant to be a guide and a jumping off tool to get you thinking about your special and important relationship with the planet. So re-engage your five senses and allow your imagination to let your mind wander. Permit your body to re-explore smells, sights, and sounds that may have gone unnoticed for years. My challenge to you is to learn to love and respect your world as much as you do yourself because that excitement and energy is contagious and it's desperately needed to save our planet. You CAN make a noticeable difference in your home, in your school, and in your community, and you should know that these changes are part of a vast youth movement around the world.

—Lauren Wechsler Horn

KEY TERMS

BIODEGRADABLE—Biodegradable material can be naturally broken down by water, air, and soil into organic components that typically do not harm the earth or contaminate the water. A biodegradable product can usually dissolve easily in the environment without destroying nature. To illustrate this point let's consider how long it takes some things to naturally degrade—an orange peel takes approximately 6 months, a tin can take up to 100 years, and a plastic bottle…well, that takes forever.

CARCINOGENIC—If something is carcinogenic it means that it has the potential to cause cancer.

FOSSIL FUELS—Fossil fuels are natural substances that have been made deep within the earth from the remains of ancient plants and animals. Over time, heat and pressure turned these decomposing remains into fuels (think gushing oil geyser), which release energy when burned. Coal, oil, and natural gas are the three main fossil fuels. The type of fossil fuels created depends on the types of plants or animals and the degree of heat and pressure. People around the world rely on fossil fuels to make electricity, drive cars, heat homes, etc. Fossil fuels supply about 90% of the world's energy. Even though fossil fuels provide us with energy we need, our dependence on them has lead to overuse and depletion. That's a problem because they take millions of years to be made and they are non renewable (meaning they won't last forever). Another problem is that to release their stored energy, fossil fuels must be burned. It is during this process that a variety of greenhouse gases and pollution are released into the atmosphere; which leads to global climate change. It's all starting to make sense, right? Lastly, there are also environmental risks associated with extracting, transporting, and utilizing fossil fuels. Mining for coal and drilling for oil are especially hazardous because the digging of massive mines and wells can change the surrounding landscapes and bring massive amounts of saltwater to the surface which can damage nearby ecosystems.

GREENHOUSE GASES AND GLOBAL WARMING—Greenhouse gases (like water vapor, carbon dioxide, ozone, and methane) present in the atmosphere reduce the loss of heat into space and therefore contribute to global temperatures. Greenhouse gases make up only about 1% of the earth's atmosphere, and they work by regulating our climate by trapping heat and holding it in—kind of like a warm blanket that surrounds the planet. Greenhouse gases are critical to maintaining the temperature of the earth; without them our planet would be so cold it would be unable to support life. But while this process is an essential environmental prerequisite for life on earth, there can really be too much of a good thing. The problems begin when human activities like deforestation, burning natural gas and oil, landfills, unchecked population growth, and the release of fumes from factories, distort and accelerate the natural process by creating more greenhouse gases in the atmosphere than are necessary to warm the planet to an ideal temperature. When this happens it's called the greenhouse effect and the results can be devastating. Temperatures rise (commonly known as Global Warming), ice caps melt, seas rise, weather patterns change, and our fragile ecological balance is in danger. Yikes!

LANDFILL—Simply put, a landfill is an open hole in the ground where all our trash is buried. Landfills are designed to prevent waste from mixing with groundwater and to reduce odors. Most well-made landfills have a thick plastic liner between the ground and the trash, and a layer of soil is added every day to cover up the trash on top. For the most part, materials deposited in a landfill do not decompose quickly and they can stay there for hundreds or thousands of years. Landfills are now thought of as the last resort in terms of waste management because they release gases that can contribute to global warming.

SUSTAINABILITY—Sustainability is the goal of using the earth's resources to meet our present needs without jeopardizing the ability of future generations to meet their own needs. For instance, a continuously maintained forest where mature trees are harvested and new trees are replanted to filter pollutants and provide continued resources and products for future generations could be called a sustainable system. In essence, replace what you use, only use what you need, and think about what your grandchildren could (or could not) have in 50 years.

VOLATILE ORGANIC COMPOUNDS OR VOCs—These are organic chemical compounds that have high enough vapor pressures under normal conditions to vaporize (turn into a gas from being a liquid or solid) and enter the atmosphere. Common artificial VOCs include paint thinners, dry cleaning solvents, and gasoline. VOCs are sometimes accidentally released into the environment, where they can damage soil and groundwater. And vapors of VOCs escaping into the air contribute to air pollution. The most common natural VOC is methane, a greenhouse gas that is naturally released from sources such as wetlands, manure, energy use, rice agriculture, and burning wood.

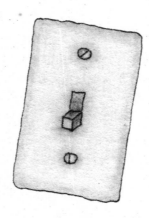

CHAPTER 1
WATER

O Don't waste your drinking water by pouring it down the sink. Instead, pour it on a nearby thirsty plant or top off your goldfish bowl.

Before leaving the bathroom or kitchen, double-check to make sure your tap is not dripping. Millions of gallons of wasted water go down the drain every day because of leaky faucets.

WOW FACT!

Here is an example of the water we use every day: 37 gallons for the toilet, 25–30 gallons for the tub, 50–70 gallons for a 10-minute shower, a washing machine load uses 25–40 gallons, and a dishwasher load uses 9–12 gallons. Try to cut down your water usage in all these areas to reduce these numbers.

WOW FACT!

There are more than 46,000 pieces of plastic waste in every square mile of the world's oceans. Recycle plastic bottles or refrain from using them altogether.

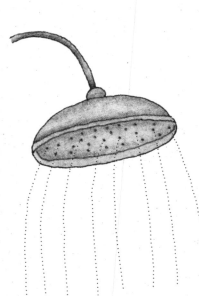

ɚ Ask your parents or the adults in your life to install a low-flow shower head in all your bathrooms. Using less water in the shower means less energy required to heat the water.

☺☺ If it's okay with your parents, consider sharing a bath with a sibling or soaping up and reusing bath water after a younger, cleaner sibling is done with his or her own bath.

✳ Before running a bath, plug the tub before you start. This saves gallons of water from going down the drain before you even get in the bath.

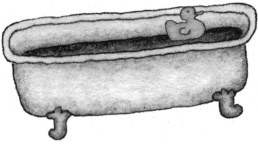

If you have more than one "bay" in your kitchen sink, fill up the empty bay with water and rinse the dishes in it instead of running water over each dish and piece of cutlery.

$ For the most part, what comes out of your tap is good quality. If you're unsure, ask an adult to install a water filter on your home faucet. A $5 filter will give you 40,000 eight-ounce glasses of purified tap water.

! To save water over time, keep a large pitcher of drinking water in the refrigerator so you don't need to continuously run the tap at each meal or snack.

WOW FACT!

We each use about 12,000 gallons of water every year. Small changes like taking shorter showers can have a huge impact.

☞ Don't load up on individual serving and overpackaged bottled water. It costs lots of money and wastes hundreds of plastic bottles per year. Instead, refill a reusable water bottle every day and take it to school.

O Suggest to your parents a good way to reduce the amount of water that gets flushed down the toilet: Place a brick or plastic bottle filled with water and rocks in your tank to reduce the amount of water used in each flush. Also, a low-flush toilet uses half the water but still does the job.

Just because you've worn it doesn't mean it's dirty. Throwing only truly dirty and smelly clothing in the washing machine means less wasted water and electricity and less work for Mom and Dad. So hang up your gently worn clothes and save water and energy.

Make your bath work double-time and save valuable water. As long as you haven't used chemical-ridden bath oils, take a bucketful of used bath water and nourish your houseplants. Do the same thing by rinsing fruits and vegetables in a bucket.

Don't use your toilet as a trash can. Toss dirty tissues, cotton balls, and Q-tips in the garbage to avoid unnecessary flushes and water waste.

WOW FACT!

Fourteen billion pounds of trash are dumped into the ocean every year. Learn about what you can do to prevent this.

When disposing of cough syrups or aspirin or other medicines, don't flush them down the toilet. Many pharmaceutical drugs end up in our drinking water, which contaminates people as well as animals and aquatic life.

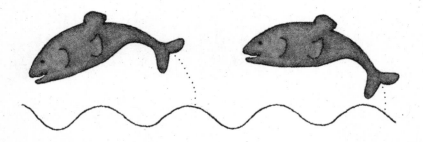

❗ If you see a leaking fire hydrant, call the local fire department to report it. By doing so you could save gallons of water.

✳ There's no need to wash your hair every day, so cut back to 3–4 days a week to save water. Washing less often is also healthier for your hair as more natural oils coat the hair shafts to give your mane a shiny sheen.

➡ Place a hair catcher in your shower so excess hair doesn't get caught in the drain. When you are finished washing, put the clump of hair in your garbage pail, not the toilet. It's better for your pipes and better for the marine life that will not end up choking on a hair ball!

⭕ Don't let your hose run in summer to cool down. Visit a neighbor's pool or a community pool instead.

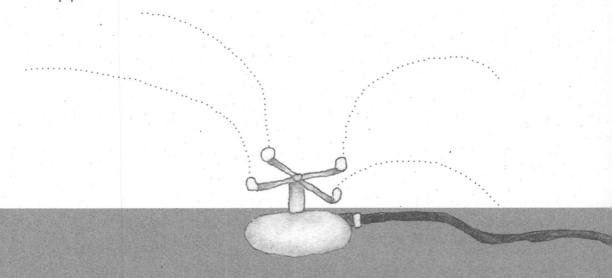

ജ For fun in the bath (remember, don't fill it to the top) use natural food dye to color the water instead of colored and fragranced bath balls.

✿ Instead of using the hose or faucet to water houseplants, catch rainwater in a small pail outside your windowsill or in your garden.

➡ Run the dishwasher and laundry machine only when the units are full.

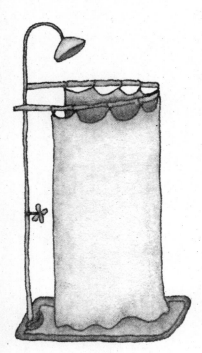

❗ When it's possible, take showers instead of baths. Showers save water heating costs and carbon dioxide (CO_2). If you take long showers, consider cutting them short by a few minutes. You'll conserve water and the electricity needed to heat up the water.

⭕ Cut down on evaporation by putting a cover on your pool. Doing so could prevent up to an inch of lost water per week.

WOW FACT!

Approximately 5 million tons of oil produced in the world each year end up in the ocean. It's important to educate yourself on the effects this has on the environment and what you can do to stop this.

✳ Ask your parents to wash the family car at a neighborhood car wash instead of at home with the hose. Believe it or not, commercial car washes maximize water conservation by recycling wash water.

$ Can't wait for the water to heat up on those cold winter mornings? Ask your parents to buy a "point of use" or "tankless" water heater that produces instant hot water, thereby reducing the amount of water you waste waiting for the flow to warm up.

WOW FACT!

The world's biggest landfill is not even in the land, it's in the Pacific Ocean. Think about the impact of this on the creatures in the ocean.

🪣 Look for water- or soy-based paints, glues, and inks. Avoid oil-based paints, turpentine, benzene, toluene, rubber cement and its thinner, and all aerosol sprays.

❀ For school and home use, seek out recycled, nonchlorine-bleached paper with high postconsumer content. Chlorine creates harmful dioxins that can seep into the groundwater.

WOW FACT!

Forty percent of all sea life has been destroyed over the last 25 years as a result of human pollution. Remember to put your trash in a garbage can, not on the beach or in the water.

🌲 If you're helping out with the laundry, use only cold water. Each load uses about 40 gallons of water, which requires a lot of energy to heat up if you're using warm or hot water. One household can eliminate more than a thousand pounds of greenhouse gas emissions per year just by washing in cold water.

❗ When brushing your teeth, wet your brush, then turn off the water. Turn the water on again to rinse your brush. Don't waste water by letting it needlessly run down the drain.

Art Project

Brighten up a shabby mirror or picture frame with seashells. After taking a long walk on the beach and collecting seashells by the seashore, sit down with an old frame and strategically glue shells around the outside. It makes for a great gift or treat for yourself and it will always remind you of the beauty of the shore and ocean.

CHAPTER 2
LAND

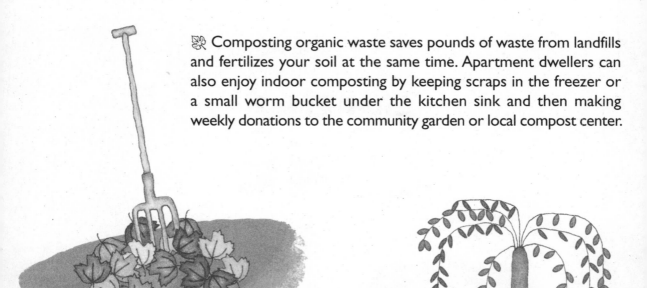

❧ Composting organic waste saves pounds of waste from landfills and fertilizes your soil at the same time. Apartment dwellers can also enjoy indoor composting by keeping scraps in the freezer or a small worm bucket under the kitchen sink and then making weekly donations to the community garden or local compost center.

WOW FACT!

If every household in the United States replaced just one box of 85-sheet virgin-fiber facial tissues with 100 percent recycled ones, we'd save 87,700 trees and 31 million gallons of water. Or, if you're not too squeamish about bodily fluids, try handkerchiefs instead.

✍ Keep yourself company with lots of houseplants. They produce oxygen, purify the air, and don't talk back.

✳ Every few rides lube your bike chain with a plant- or vegetable-based lubricant, like soy. Biodegradable lubricants and waxes are also good for maintaining snowboards, skis, surfboards, and wake boards. They're just as good as the conventional petrochemical waxes, but when they end up in the groundwater they're not as dangerous.

Art Project

Twig Vase: On your next nature walk, trip to the park, or walk to school, take time to collect some long, straight twigs for a nature-inspired vase.

Twigs
Rubber bands
One empty glass jar
Twine or ribbon
Glue

1. Break your twigs so that they are an inch longer than the height of the glass jar.
2. Wrap a rubber band around the neck of the jar, about an inch from the top.
3. Wrap another band around the jar, an inch from the bottom.
4. Place the twigs around the jar, tucking the ends under both rubber bands to hold twigs in place. Space them as closely as possible.
5. When the jar is covered with twigs, slide the rubber bands toward each other, so that they meet in the middle of the jar.
6. Squeeze some glue near the top of the project between the twigs and the glass. Let dry.
7. Turn jar upside down and repeat step 6.
8. Turn right side up and wrap a few pieces of twine or ribbon around the top and bottom of the jar, leaving about an inch from the top and bottom.
9. To finish the vase off, snip off the rubber bands.

Landfills are the biggest emitters of the greenhouse gas methane and there are higher incidences of cancer and other diseases among people living near them. If landfills do leak, leachate—a toxic substance—is released into the groundwater and soil, meaning local drinking water could get contaminated. Reduce your waste to make a difference.

➡ In traditional dry cleaning, clothes are doused with a cancer-causing chemical called perchloroethylene, or "perc," which can contaminate soil. Opt for greener alternatives like wet cleaning or liquid CO_2 dry cleaning. Or just avoid clothes that require dry cleaning in the first place.

🌱 Pesticides used in lawn care kill as many as 70 million birds every year in the United States, can run off into groundwater and beyond, killing sea life, and have been linked to birth defects. So tell your adults to use natural weed killers, because they make for healthier soil and because they don't harm the way chemical herbicides do.

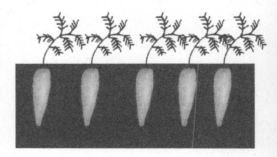

Art Project

Potpourri Pinecones: Spend a crisp fall day walking outside and collecting pinecones for yummy-smelling botanical potpourri.

Newspapers
½ cup glue
½ cup water
Cinnamon, cloves, nutmeg, or other spices
Paintbrush
Pinecones
Mixing bowl and spoon
Plastic bowl(s) (one for each spice)
Small basket or decorative bowl

1. Lay newspapers over the entire work area.

2. Mix the glue and water together in the mixing bowl.

3. Put each spice into its plastic bowl.

4. Using the paintbrush, coat an entire pinecone with a layer of the glue mixture.

5. Now, roll the pinecone in one or more different spices. Be sure to cover the entire pinecone.

6. Repeat steps 4 and 5 for each potpourri pinecone you want to make.

7. Set the pinecones aside to dry for several hours.

8. Display your pinecones in a small basket or decorative bowl, and they'll keep your home smelling sweet and woodsy.

🪣 For house painting and art projects use acrylic paint instead of oil-based paints, which are toxic and create pollution during manufacturing. Also look for paints that meet the EPA's low-VOC (volatile organic compounds) standards or, better yet, ones with the Green Seal label.

🌳 Instead of playing online video games, plant a tree with some friends. Over time, more trees in your community can make a big difference. Trees clean the air by intercepting airborne particles and absorbing such pollutants as carbon monoxide, sulfur dioxide, and nitrogen dioxide. Can your Game Boy do all that?

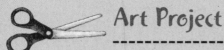

Art Project

Flower Petal Stained Glass: Brighten up any window by pinning up a homemade stained-glass design. You will need an adult's help with the ironing.

Flower petals and small leaves
Wooden Popsicle sticks
Wax paper
Crayon pieces
Paper clips
Kitchen towel
Iron

1. Search for and collect an assortment of flower petals and small, colorful leaves. Remember to collect only those petals which have already fallen to the ground.

2. Using a Popsicle stick, scrape crayon pieces over a paper towel to make a handful of crayon shavings. Use different colors that complement the flower petals.

3. Cut two foot-long pieces of wax paper.

4. Arrange the petals on one sheet of wax paper however you want.

5. Sprinkle the crayon shavings on the wax paper in between the petals and leaves.

6. Place the other piece of wax paper on top of the flower petals and crayon shavings. Secure the sheets together with paper clips.

7. Place a kitchen towel over the wax paper. Have your mom or dad set the iron on low heat and iron over the towel.

8. Display your new stained glass in a window.

WOW FACT!

Cities cover only 2 percent of the earth's surface but their populations consume 75 percent of the planet's agricultural resources such as food. But even city dwellers can grow things—learn about urban gardens in your area.

❗ Encourage your school board or your apartment's management to create a rooftop garden. These gardens help clean the air and they also provide insulation for both heating and cooling.

🌹 If you don't have a big backyard, make an organic urban garden instead. Urban gardens—little gardens on vacant lots, rooftops, terraces, or balconies—are fun to take care of and great for growing herbs for all your family dinners.

WOW FACT!

The Amazon rain forest loses 2,000 trees per minute. That's enough to fill seven football fields. To cut down on the amount of paper used in the classroom, encourage your teacher to use both sides of the paper for handouts.

Participate in or organize a community clean-up project. Cleaning up a local beach, street, park, playground, or lake can help keep wildlife healthy and can increase neighborhood pride.

If you go to the beach or a park or are just plain hiking around in the woods, leave it cleaner than how you found it. Pick up cans and other trash that were there when you arrived.

WOW FACT!

The United States has less than 4 percent of its original forests left. Use recycled paper whenever possible to help decrease this statistic.

Art Project

Ladybug Paperweights: Brighten up your home or your teacher's desk by collecting rocks and making them into paperweights.

Several smooth, round, or oval rocks, washed and dried
Water-based craft paints (including black) and paintbrush
Black marker
Two wiggle eyes for each ladybug (optional)
Glue (optional)

1. Completely wash and dry all rocks.

2. Paint rocks in desired colors, and allow them to dry. Apply second and third coats if needed. Lighter colors will require more coats than darker shades.

3. Paint head using black paint. There is no pattern needed, simply paint about ¼ of the rock black in the "front."

4. Use a black marker to draw a straight line down the center of the rock, starting at the center of the base of the "head."

5. Dip the handle of a large paintbrush, or the eraser of a pencil, in black paint. Dot on the spots, reloading with paint after making each dot.

6. Once the paint is dry; seal your creation with diluted glue (approximately three parts glue to one part water).

7. Let dry and glue on wiggle eyes as desired.

CHAPTER 3
ENERGY

⚠️ A great deal of the resources we use and the waste we create is in the energy we consume. Your family can look for opportunities to reduce their energy use. For example, take public transportation instead of driving, fly less, turn off lights, wear a sweater instead of turning up the heat, use a clothesline instead of a dryer, go camping instead of staying in a hotel, buy used items or borrow things before buying new, and recycle.

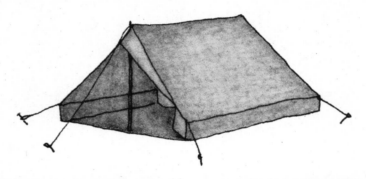

WOW FACT!

More than ⅓ of all energy is used by people at home. Hand washing at least some clothes helps out around the house and saves electricity.

🌱 To change things around, ask your parents to use candles instead of turning on the lights. And choose veggie-based pillar candles (such as soy-based candles) instead of the petroleum-based ones. The label should list the ingredients.

Art Project

Homemade Soy Candles: You can never go wrong with pesticide- and herbicide-free soy candles. They're biodegradable and will spice up any room. And if you choose to make one as a present, you'll literally be giving the gift of light. Ask an adult to help you with the cooking part of this craft. Makes one or two medium-sized candles.

Scissors
One package braided hemp wick
Reused glass jars, candy dishes, or thrift-store cups
Soda can tab
Glue
Pencils or pens
Tape

Tin melting pot or an old cookpot, just for candle making
One pound soy wax flakes
Candle- or candy-making thermometer (optional)
Large spoon
Cinnamon essential oil
Biodegradable cotton ribbon (optional)

1. Cut a section of braided wick a few inches longer than the depth of your chosen glass container. Tie an end of the wick to a soda can tab. To stabilize the wick, add a dab of glue to the bottom of the tab, then affix tab to the bottom of the container. Wrap top of wick around a pencil or pen a few times so that the wick is taut and the pen is resting on the mouth of the container. Tape the pen temporarily in place and set jar aside. Repeat process for additional containers.

2. In a pot over medium heat, have your parents help melt soy flakes. Stir continuously until soy wax melts to about 155 degrees. Once it's completely liquefied, remove it from heat and let cool for a few minutes, continuing to stir.

3. Once the temperature has dropped to about 150 degrees, add 10–20 drops of cinnamon essential oil and mix well.

4. Pour liquid wax into containers, leaving an inch or two of space at the top. Let cool overnight. The candle wax should look smooth and creamy white.

5. Remove tape and pencil from wick. Leaving about 1" of exposed wick, snip off the excess.

6. If you're giving these candles as gifts, you could decorate them by tying biodegradable cotton ribbon and gluing it to the glass, or by gluing a piece of ribbon around the rim.

✳ When it comes time for you and your family to choose a new computer, go with a laptop. They use as much as 90 percent less energy than desktop computers. They run on rechargeable batteries, and have energy-saving features like low-energy display screens and automatic sleep modes.

$ Instead of constantly running a screensaver, set the computer to go to sleep mode. Doing so can save $25–$75 per desktop every year on your parents' power bills.

☞ To save energy, always turn off the lights when you leave a room or go to sleep for the night.

☾ No one likes feeling scared at night, so talk to your parents about getting you or your siblings an energy-saving night-light.

☼ In one day, the sun provides more energy than our population could use in 27 years. Switch to natural sunlight instead of using electric lamps during the day.

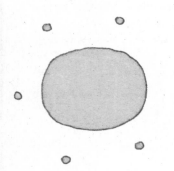

❗ Ask the adults in your home to turn down the temperature on the water heater. Most homes have their water heater's thermostat turned up too high, wasting energy. Turn it down to 130 degrees, saving energy but still hot enough to kill bacteria.

Always cover pots to speed up cooking, because the less time it takes, the more energy you conserve. The trapped steam encourages the pot's ingredients to cook faster.

Give your computer a bedtime by shutting it off when it's not in use for long periods of time. Contrary to popular belief, turning PCs off overnight does not wear them out. But it does save hundreds of pounds of CO_2 emissions per year.

Just like you have yearly doctor visits, your family car needs an annual checkup as well. Keeping your family's car in good working condition will not only make it last longer, it will make it more fuel efficient.

Remind your parents to inflate the family car tires every few weeks. Properly inflated tires will reduce fuel consumption and make the tires last longer. The amount of air the tire needs is written right on it.

WOW FACT!

The 500 million automobiles on Earth burn an average of two gallons of fuel a day. Hybrid cars are much more environmentally friendly and their greater use would significantly reduce this figure.

➡ Ask the adults in your life to combine running errands for efficiency. Help them plan their schedule and route to cut down on fuel consumption and possibly even their valuable time.

$ Ask permission to walk, ride your bike or scooter, or carpool to school. It saves on fuel consumption, cuts your fuel spending, reduces greenhouse emissions, gets you in shape, and you can talk with your friends!

WOW FACT!

Each gallon of fuel releases 20 pounds of carbon dioxide into the air, which contributes to the "greenhouse effect." Walk or ride your bike as much as possible.

✳ You and your siblings have power. When your family goes to buy a new vehicle, ask your parents to be included in the discussion. Ask your mom or dad to consider a more fuel-efficient car or a hybrid, which can reduce smog by 90 percent compared with even the cleanest vehicles on the road today.

📺 Turn off the TV and read a book or play a board game. Or go outside and take a walk, play tag or hide-and-seek, or meet up with your friends instead. It's guaranteed to be more fun and burns less fossil fuels.

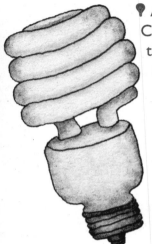

💡 Ask adults to replace old incandescent light bulbs with fluorescent CFL bulbs (those spiral-looking ones). They last up to 10 times longer than regular bulbs and the energy savings is great. However, because CFLs contain low levels of mercury (less than in old-time thermometers), recycling is a must. They should not be tossed in the garbage bin or put out with regular recycling, and caution should be taken if one breaks. Check your local sanitation department for recycling options.

❗ More and more local utility companies are giving customers the option to choose alternative and renewable sources of energy (like water and wind generated), so ask your parents to look into it. If your power company isn't one that offers green power, they might offer renewable-energy certificates to support green energy providers. Green energy costs a little bit more, but the power releases no CO_2 into the atmosphere.

✮ When it's time to replace certain outdated, energy-sucking, water-wasting appliances in your house, like washing machines and dishwashers, tell your parents to look for ENERGY STAR appliances. Your parents can end up saving thousands of gallons of water and thousands of dollars on energy bills over the lifetime of the appliance.

🐁 Ever wonder why you still see a red light on appliances and electronics even when you know they're turned off? That's because as long as cell phone chargers, phones, toasters, computers, TVs, DVRs, and iPod chargers are plugged into the wall they are still using electricity. Unplugging them is the only way to ensure that they are not sucking up energy, especially when you're away for a long weekend or are traveling on vacation.

❗ Make your parents happy and clean out all your sports equipment from the family's car. Do you really need ice skates and beach chairs in there when they're not in season? Cleaning out the clutter and weight inside the car increases its fuel economy by 1 to 2 percent. So if you don't need it on the trip you're taking, don't have it in your trunk.

✳ If you get picked up at school, remind your mom, dad, or babysitter not to idle while they wait. Idling wastes money and gas, and generates pollution and global warming–causing emissions.

➡ Ask the cook in your family to defrost foods in the refrigerator instead of on the countertop. The frozen food will help keep the rest of the fridge cold, reducing the energy needed to run it. And you'll save the energy you would have spent defrosting in the microwave or oven.

📺 If your family is in the market for a new TV, remember that LCDs (liquid crystal displays) use the least energy of the leading screen types, followed by plasma screens. Old-fashioned CRT (cathode ray tube) televisions use the most power.

It doesn't take as much energy to reheat food as it does to cook it in the first place, so help your parents make enough food for next-day leftovers.

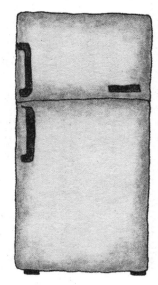

Don't stand with the fridge door open while you decide what you want. When you do, cold air rushes out and warm air takes its place. The fridge then uses extra electricity to cool back down. Instead decide first; then open, grab, and shut. Challenge your family to do the same.

Air travel is a major contributor to pollution. Reduce your family's carbon footprint by asking to be included in vacation planning. Suggest you go somewhere by train or bus or consider staying closer to home and enjoy more time recreating and less in transit.

$ Help cut your family's energy costs by closing doors to rooms that you rarely go in and out of on a regular basis. This makes sure the hot (or cold) air stays where you need it and not where you don't.

If your family is into water sports, suggest they look into electricity-powered small crafts or boats that use biodiesel as the fuel of choice.

Remind your parents to clean the filters on heating and air-conditioning units to keep them operating efficiently. Dirty filters require your units to use more energy as they work harder.

➡ Surprise your mom and dad by cleaning the lint filter in your dryer after each use to help keep it working effectively.

❢ Do a lightbulb check to make sure that no dust has accumulated on the tops. Dirty bulbs emit less light and can make you think you need a higher wattage bulb when you really don't.

WOW FACT!

The energy we save when we recycle one glass bottle is enough to light a traditional lightbulb for four hours.

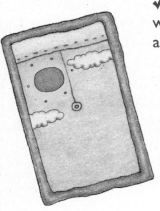

✔ Find out if your home needs storm windows. They provide additional insulation and reduce heating and cooling costs.

🔺 Planting big shade trees outside your home can reduce the temperature inside by 10 to 20 degrees, and save your family about $200 a year in electricity.

CHAPTER 4
ANIMALS

❗ Even if spiders creep you out, don't squish them. There are an estimated 40,000 species of spiders, and they all eat insects. Spiders are an important part of the food web and provide natural pest control as they eat pesky bugs.

🐾 Always scoop your pet's waste when you take him or her on walks. If possible, pick it up with a paper bag or old newspaper. Otherwise, your pooch's waste could sit inside a plastic bag in a landfill for hundreds of years.

🐕 As long as you're going green, convert your dog as well. When it's time to buy him or her a new leash and collar, try a hemp variety that does not contain pesticides. While you're at it, throw in a comfy pet bed without any harmful chemical additives in it.

🐈 Green your kitty by switching to biodegradable litter, which is often made from renewable plant resources, and can include recycled newspaper, wood pellets, sawdust, corn cobs, dried orange peel, or wheat bran. Biodegradable litter can be safely eliminated by composting or flushing it straight down the toilet.

➡ Do your research and don't buy pet food from companies that conduct animal force-feeding tests.

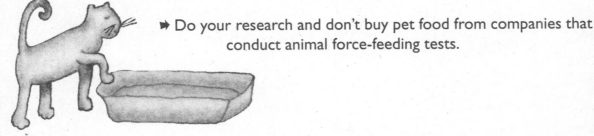

Art Project

Pinecone Bird Feeder: Let your art go to the birds by making a gourmet feeder for them. Makes four bird feeders.

4 pinecones
Old newspapers
Popsicle stick
1 cup peanut butter
2 cups oatmeal or birdseed (mixed variety)
String or yarn cut into 4-foot strips

1. Take a walk and collect an assortment of pinecones.

2. Place old newspapers on the work surface where you'll be making your bird feeders.

3. Using a Popsicle stick, spread 1/4 of peanut butter all over each pinecone. Be sure to cover the surface completely.

4. Spread out birdseed and oatmeal in two different piles on top of the newspapers.

5. Roll two of the pinecones in the birdseed until they're completely coated and no peanut butter is visible. Do the same thing with the other two pinecones in the oatmeal pile.

6. Tie a piece of string around the top of each pinecone.

7. Ask an adult to hang the pinecones from tree branches in your yard or outside your apartment building.

8. Look out your window and see which birds like the birdseed and which like the oatmeal.

WOW FACT!

Each year, more than 2 million tons of cat litter, or approximately 100,000 truckloads, ends up in landfills in the United States alone. Primarily this is not biodegradable or renewable and adds unnecessarily to the waste burden. Consider training your cat to go to the bathroom outdoors or using biodegrable litter.

❗ Don't assume that everything associated with the word organic must be good for your pet. Even organic chocolate can be poisonous to cats and dogs.

🦋 Avoid the impulse to pick beautiful wildflowers while on a hike or nature walk. By leaving them in the ground, others can enjoy them, and bees can feed from them too.

Paint or number the shells of snails in your garden (using nontoxic paint, of course) so you can follow each one of their exploits to see how and where they live. What do they do all day long? Where do they forage for food? What do they eat?

Before you throw out plastic six-pack rings, cut all the circles with a scissor so birds and animals don't get their bodies or necks stuck in them.

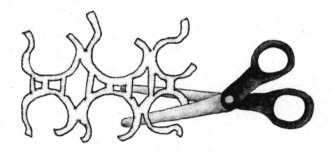

WOW FACT!

Plastic bags littered in and around aquatic environments kill at least 100,000 birds, whales, seals, and turtles every year. Pick up any loose litter you see and dispose of it properly.

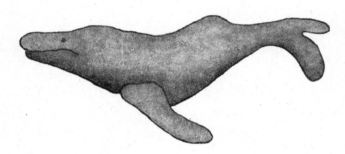

Don't let your family rely on zappers, sonic devices, or carbon monoxide traps to keep from getting bitten by mosquitoes. Zappers kill mostly larger, beneficial insects, which eat mosquitoes. Instead, wear long sleeves and use natural repellants, which typically use lemon and eucalyptus derivatives.

➡ Saying no to wearing fur and animal products is not a fashion death wish. Be creative and expand your look to include all-natural fibers such as bamboo and vintage styles.

Art Project

Bird House: To go along with your new bird feeders, recycle an empty milk carton to make a bird sanctuary. An adult should help with the cutting.

A gallon-size plastic milk jug, empty and clean
Sharp knife
Old cloth, straw, or shredded paper
12" dowel stick
Rope or heavy lanyard

1. After cleaning the jug, place the lid back on it.

2. Once the carton is completely dry, have your parents take the sharp knife and cut a circle in the middle of the carton on two opposite sides. Make the holes about 1 to 1 ½ inches in diameter. Birds like holes that fit their size.

3. You can put little bits of torn-up clean cloth, straw, or paper in the carton to help the birds start their nest.

4. Put little holes underneath the larger holes so you can slide the dowel through the smaller holes. This will be the perch where the birds will land when they come home.

5. Hang your house with rope or a lanyard, where you can see the neighborhood birds come and go.

6. This craft also makes a good feeder. Instead of putting torn-up cloth on the bottom, pour in birdseed and watch the locals feast.

🐦 Put out a bird feeder or nesting box in your yard or near your school to enjoy seasonal birds. Birds also get rid of pesky insects, so you're helping the circle of life.

❗Resist the urge to feed cute animals and birds with human food. Doing so can interfere with their natural foraging instincts and can also negatively affect their migratory patterns.

🖌 Always try to use synthetic art brushes instead of ones made from animal hair.

CHAPTER 5

REDUCE, REUSE, RECYCLE

➥ Get to know your plastics. There are two main groups: thermoplastics and thermosets. Thermoplastics (like acrylic, Teflon, and polyvinyl chloride) soften with heat and harden with cooling and are in your clothing, raingear, and other products. Thermosets (like epoxy and polyester) also are in some clothing as well as products like glue, markers, and water bottles. Plastic uses tons of oil and other chemicals during manufacturing. It does not biodegrade easily and can leak toxic chemicals into foods and groundwater.

WOW FACT!

If everybody consumed at U.S. rates, we would need 3 to 5 planets. The average U.S. person now consumes twice as much as he did 50 years ago. Think about the impact your consumption has on the planet as a whole.

Americans generate about 4.6 pounds of solid trash per day—twice as much as 30 years ago. This adds up to big trouble for the environment because we are generating waste products faster than nature can break them down, and we are using up resources faster than they can be replaced. The easiest way to help the planet is to reduce your waste output by consuming and throwing away less stuff.

❗ Glass can be recycled again and again without losing its clarity or purity.

🥤 Be sure to cross foam cups off your family's shopping list. With the amount of foam cups Americans use each year, we could circle the earth 436 times.

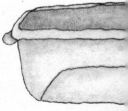

O Because one quart of motor oil can contaminate 250,000 gallons of water, it's important to make sure your parents know how to recycle their used motor vehicle oils. Most service stations, repair facilities, and quick lubes will accept used oil without charge.

✳ As an experiment, weigh your trash. First, collect bins to sort your household waste. You might want to use the following categories: "paper," "metal," "plastic," "glass," "food," and "other." Over the course of a week, place each item of trash in the proper bin. On the last day, weigh each bag to determine how big of an impact your family makes each week. Then sit down and think about how to cut down on your family's output. Look at some of the containers that you are throwing out and come up with other uses for them and also look at the amount

of food waste collected and consider composting it (meat, dairy, and high-fat items are not good for composting).

✳ A little known fact of recycling is that none of your recyclables need to be completely spotless since most "contaminants" get cleaned out or burned away during remanufacturing. So save some water and don't overrinse your recyclables.

WOW FACT!

Every steel can is 100 percent recyclable. It can be recycled over and over again into products like bicycles and, of course, new cans.

🔩 Search for used sports equipment (bikes, skis, skates, hockey equipment) that is well made and durable instead of buying less expensive but poorer quality new stuff.

✳ Have the adults you know buy minimally packaged products. Doing so could reduce your garbage by about 10 percent and save 1,200 pounds of carbon dioxide and $1,000 per year.

✔ Avoid products that are packaged for single-serving use. Instead of using tiny packets of sugar, blisters of mustard, or small pouches of pet food, buy in bulk and redistribute to smaller-use containers.

👄 Resist the power of cute and think before you buy unnecessary "stuff" that will probably land up in the garbage in a few months. Do you really need that new barrette or lip gloss?

Art Project

Toothbrush Bracelet (or Napkin Rings): Start a new fashion trend by turning your old, flat toothbrush into a unique recycled piece of jewelry. An adult will need to help you with this whole project.

Old flat toothbrush
Tweezers or pliers
Pot tongs
Large mug
Oven mitts

1. Remove all the bristles from the toothbrush using tweezers or pliers.

2. In a pot large enough to hold the entire length of your toothbrush, boil water at a depth that covers the toothbrush bristles.

3. Boil submerged toothbrush for five minutes.

4. Remove toothbrush with tongs and carefully bend to desired shape. If the toothbrush doesn't bend enough, submerge again in water.

5. Remove brush and bend as much as possible. Place bent toothbrush in the bottom of a mug to hold its shape while it cools. Pour cold water in the mug, then remove your new bracelet.

Instead of buying new jewelry and accessories, buy used. You can get them at funky secondhand shops and consignment stores for cheaper, and still get quality—all the while reducing the need to produce more stuff.

❗ Set up a plastic bag recycling program in your apartment building. Put a box of plastic bags in your building's lobby so people can grab one on their way out to shop or walk the dog. Plastic bags are not the greenest choice, but at least you'll be encouraging reuse and reducing consumer need.

WOW FACT!

There are more than 100,000 synthetic chemicals in commerce today. Use natural products in place of manmade ones.

✂ Worn scissors and shears are typically discarded, but almost all of them, including those that are severely abused, can be restored and used again, at prices much lower than purchasing new ones. Reconditioning virtually renews used scissors, so don't toss your garden shears. Just get them tuned up instead.

👖 Americans tend to discard their outdated jeans as trends and styles change, but old pairs can be cut into shorts, made into book covers or bags, used as cleaning rags, worn for yard work, or tied in a knot and used as a pet's chew toy. In fact, if you keep them around for another 15 years they'll probably go back in style again.

✔ Buy vintage clothes. You'll look unique and hip with combinations from different eras and styles while keeping the cancer-linked petrochemicals used in garment "sizing" out of the environment and water supply.

Art Project

CD Locker Magnet: Spruce up the inside of your locker using old CDs.

5 wallet-sized school photos
Old CD
White glue
15–20 round craft jewels (or buttons, beads, or coins) in various colors
1 medium-sized square craft jewel
3 round magnets

1. Trim photos to fit on the CD. Arrange them and glue in place.

2. Glue round craft jewels around the edge of the CD to frame it. Allow to dry completely.

3. Glue magnets to the back of the CD and hang in your locker.

✳ Don't get sucked into buying trendy, cheap, and disposable goods. Instead look for long-lasting, well-made, durable, and timeless products. Look for things that have a warranty or guarantee. If it needs fixing, you can send it back for repair instead of buying a new one.

☞ Reusing items instead of using disposable ones is always a better thing for the environment. So work with your parents to turn your lunch box into a sustainable feast and waste-free meal. Use washable cloth napkins instead of paper, a stainless steel thermos instead of juice boxes or water bottles, stainless steel cutlery instead of plastic, a reusable sandwich holder instead of tinfoil and a disposable baggie. Doing all this on a daily basis reduces deforestation and toxins, and doesn't contribute to more nonbiodegradable landfill trash.

⌂ If space allows in your home, suggest that your family buy in bulk. It reduces the need for overpackaging and generally costs less.

WOW FACT!

Packaging accounts for 10-15 percent (sometimes more than 50 percent) of the cost of manufacturing a product and 50 percent of all consumer waste. Think before you buy something just because it comes in a pretty package.

$ Talk to your parents about why buying recycled products is a good thing for the environment and your family's bank account.

👣 Ask to go food shopping with your mom, dad, or grandparent so you can teach them how to prevent waste and reduce their carbon footprint. Instead of single-serving yogurts or puddings, buy the larger 32- or 64-ounce containers and scoop your daily portion into a reusable container at home. That reusable container could even be the old 6-ounce yogurt containers that you used to buy.

WOW FACT!

In the United States, we spend 3-4 times as many hours shopping as our counterparts in Europe do. More shopping leads to more consumption, so find other activities to do instead.

💲 Recycle everything that can be recycled and cut down on the things that cannot. Contact your local sanitation department to find out the list of items that can and cannot be recycled. If you recycle by donating items to charity, they are tax deductions for your family too.

WOW FACT!

Americans use about 57 billion pounds of plastic a year—and recycle only 3 percent of it. Each piece recycled makes a difference.

🌴 Instead of automatically hitting the PRINT button on your home and school computer, think of whether you really need a hardcopy of that document. Can you e-mail it instead? File it on your computer instead of in your file cabinet? Read it on the computer instead of on paper? You don't have to eliminate printing entirely, but holding off on that PRINT button once in a while could greatly reduce your paper consumption.

🍳 Use reusable glass food containers to store leftovers or other food in the fridge and cabinets, instead of disposable material like tinfoil and small zip-seal plastic bags.

❋ Reuse paper that's already been printed on. Flip old homework assignments over and use the clean sides for notes or even for writing down phone messages and to-do lists.

WOW FACT!

Only 30 percent of newspapers are recycled in the United States. Knock on your neighbors' doors and ask them to recycle their papers.

☺ Ask your teachers if you can turn in homework assignments by e-mail, whenever possible, instead of printing it out.

 ♫ When you buy used CDs, books, games, and clothes, you save money. When you sell your old stuff, you get money back. When you donate your old toys and appliances, you're giving someone else a present. Pretty simple and economical, right?

🥕 Have your mom or dad use glass instead of plastic for food storage. Plastic packaging may leave chemical residues on foods stored or, especially, heated in it.

✻ Because plastic containers can leach toxins into drinks, ask for a reusable metal bottle to cart around water and juice.

✿ Use soft baby wash cloths instead of disposable cotton balls to clean and tone your face.

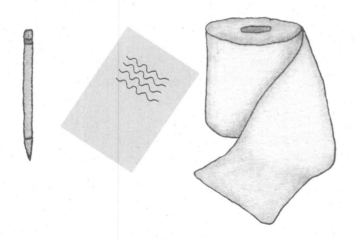

🖊 Urge your school officials to buy only recycled pencils, paper, and toilet paper. Get them to also install electric hand dryers in the bathrooms instead of paper towels.

WOW FACT!

Making disposable plastic bags requires energy equal to 4 million barrels of oil a year, and brown paper bags use up 14 million trees annually. Use reusable rather than disposable bags to carry your lunch.

❗ Buy used school books. They're cheaper and, by doing so, you send the message to others that reusing is the way to go.

✎ Make mini notepads for you and your whole family by cutting used computer paper in quarters. They're great for jotting down phone messages and using as study flash cards.

☞ When playing board games such as Pictionary use mini white boards with erasable markers. Each player can get his or her own reusable board without wasting one sheet of paper.

💡 When you're ready to upgrade, donate your computer. Not only does it keep potentially hazardous materials out of landfills, it also puts a computer in the hands of someone who needs it. Search the EPA Web site for local computer-recycling programs.

Art Project

Natural Finger Paints: Why waste time, fuel, and excessive packaging searching for the perfect finger-paint set when you can make one at home with no fuss? Ask an adult to boil the water.

$1/3$ cup soap flakes melted with $1/2$ cup boiling water
$1/2$ cup cold water
1 cup cornstarch
Juice dyes (see recipe page 99)

1. Make your own soap flakes by grating a bar of homemade hand soap until you have $1/3$ of a cup of soap flakes.

2. Melt the soap flakes in $1/2$ cup boiling water.

3. Combine the cornstarch, water, and melted soap in a bowl. Stir to blend. Let the mixture set until it has become cool and thick.

4. Divide into separate bowls and stir in juice dyes for color.

❗ When you run out of printer ink for your computer, recycle your ink cartridge at a local school or office supply store.

👕 Don't toss your stained and torn play clothes. Instead, turn them into rags for dusting and cleaning.

👕 Have your relatives save stained and old dress shirts so you can make them into smocks for when you're painting and gluing.

💵 Have a toy and game swap party with your friends. Look around your room and clean out all the old (not broken!) toys. Hold a party where everyone brings the things they don't play with anymore and go "shopping" for new toys.

➥ Don't just spare a square. Use only as much toilet paper as you really need. Americans use 400 million miles of toilet paper each year. Also look for recycled rolls that are both soft and earth friendly.

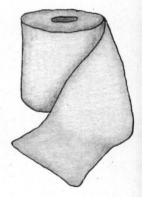

💲 Help your parents make the switch to online bill paying with their bank. If all American households received account statements online and paid their bills electronically, it would eliminate more than 800,000 tons of waste each year.

✔ Old tires can be reused and recycled in so many ways. They can be reused as swings or mini gardens, or they can be recycled and made into jar openers and playground flooring.

✿ Instead of tossing your take-out food plastic containers, wash them and keep them as storage for beads, stickers, and other small crafts. Go a step further and ask the restaurant to switch to organic waxed cardboard containers instead.

✹ Remind your parents to suspend newspaper delivery when you are out of town. This prevents a pileup of papers that will most likely never be read.

Art Project

Recycling Crayons: Have you ever thought about how many perfectly good, but stubby, crayons you will throw out over the course of your life? Put an end to the untimely demise of your crayons and recycle all your broken ones into fun shapes by creating brand-new ones. Ask an adult for help on this one.

Crayon stubs
Old saucepan or tin can for melting crayons
Assorted cookie cutters, old muffin tins, or candy molds
Aluminum foil

1. Take the paper off of the crayons and put them in an old saucepan. Or put the crayons in a clean tin can and place the can in a saucepan of water.

2. Melt the wax by turning the stove on low heat.

3. Place the cookie cutters on a sheet of aluminum foil. Pour the melted wax into assorted cookie cutters or muffin tin. You may need to hold the cookie cutters down to keep the melted wax from running out.

4. Wait for the wax to set, then cool, and pop your brand-new crayons out to use.

☺☺ When you visit new places—a museum or landmark for instance—don't take a brochure unless you really need one. Instead, share with the person sitting next to you and return it on your way out so someone else can use it after you have left.

💲 If you're allowed to shop online (make sure you have your parents' permission), rather than have each item shipped separately as soon as it becomes available, select the option that groups your order into as few shipments as possible. It might take a few days longer, but it saves on packaging and delivery-truck fuel.

 ➡ There are many different kinds of plastics, but they can be easily sorted into one of seven categories. Each type has particular properties that make it suitable for various recycling applications and are identified with a number inside a triangle on the bottom of most containers. Plastics labeled with 1 or 2 are most easily recycled, while those numbered 5, 6, and 7 are more difficult to recycle.

💡 The next time adults need nails or tape or paint, ask them to visit the local hardware store instead of a large home-improvement superstore. It saves on fuel, and a dollar spent in a locally owned business is worth three times as much to the local economy as one spent in a chain store.

♻ Approximately 27 million trees a year are destroyed to support the paper towel industry, so clean up your spills, kitchen counters, and arts and crafts messes using a cotton rag or cut-up old T-shirts instead.

✔ Plastic can only be recycled a limited number of times, so do your best to avoid food and toy packaging that uses excessive plastic.

Art Project

Memo Board: Design your family's message center by making a customized and recycled memo board. To make a tackboard, use two pieces of cardboard or use cork between the cardboard pieces.

Heavy cardboard, any size
Old fabric or wallpaper
Glue
Ribbon
Tape
Scissors

1. Wrap the cardboard with a piece of old pillowcase fabric or cut-up clothes, or scraps of leftover wallpaper.

2. Glue the overlapping pieces on all four sides to the back of the cardboard.

3. Wrap pieces of ribbon diagonally across the front of the board crisscrossing them in the middle and at the four corners.

4. Glue the ribbon to the back of the board. (Or you can tape the ends of the ribbon to hold it in place until the glue dries.)

5. Glue two pieces of ribbon on the back of the board near the top. (Make sure each piece is long enough to tie into a bow from which to hang your board.) Glue a piece of material to cover the back of the board. (Note: To hold your notes, slip pieces of paper under ribbons.)

🌲 Americans throw away 44 million newspapers every day. That's 500,000 trees a week, which is a good reason to recycle your family's paper or urge your parents to read it online.

🚲 When you've grown out of your beloved bicycle, hand it down to a younger sibling or cousin or donate it to a local children's organization.

💲 When your family is ready to buy a new couch, chair, or other large piece of furniture, consider donating the item to your school's theater department or community stage instead of tossing it to the curb.

🎸 When you go to a play or concert, on your way out return your playbills or programs to the stack or the person you got them from, instead of dumping them in the trash the minute you walk out of the theater.

💡 Organize a used book drive at your school or community center. Proceeds can support a local environmental group or can buy more recycling garbage bins.

★ Develop a toy swap with your cousins every few months instead of having your relatives buy you new gadgets.

➡ Some individual drink pouches, juice boxes, and plastic straws are difficult to recycle. Instead buy juice in bulk and fill up your thermos for lunch, at snack time, and during sports practice.

🌲 Each year, 100 million trees are used to produce junk mail like brochures, catalogs, and phone books. Find out how to get your parents off marketers' lists. In the United States 34 pounds of paper junk mail is sent to each person per year.

❗ Take a reusable, organic, cotton tote bag wherever you go and decline plastic and paper bags at grocery stores and pharmacies. If items are small enough, you can even put purchases into your school backpack or your mom's purse. Using your own bag reduces waste and requires no additional energy.

🍴 The thin, clear plastic take-out food containers that have the lid attached make great terrariums, just throw in some soil (or even a wet paper towel) add some birdseed or beans and water, close, and over time you can see that the water evaporates, and then "rains" back down. You can see the seeds sprout up, and by looking at the bottom, you can see the roots grow down. We don't recommend growing penicillin, however.

☞ Americans toss out more than 100 million cell phones every year. Keep their toxic ingredients (including lead, mercury, and arsenic) out of landfills by donating your old cell or contacting the manufacturer to find out where they recommend recycling.

◎ When you're looking for books to read, visit your school or local library or borrow books from a friend. It's great to support local businesses, but how many books do you really need to own?

✿ How many parts of your outfit could be green? Take a look at your shirt and if you see and feel nylon and polyester, you should know that these manmade fabrics release dangerous fossil fuel during manufacturing. Unnatural synthetics are an eco-fashion "don't," so keep your eye out for natural fabrics, like wool, hemp, organic cotton, and bamboo (which is lightweight and quick drying).

♥ Consider trying cutting-edge and eco-friendly fabrics made from soy and recycled soda bottles (which, as you can imagine, is especially durable).

👢 Invest in shoes that use vegetable-tanned leather or organic materials, like canvas or cotton. Once they are worn out, get them resoled instead of buying a new pair.

✏ When it's back-to-school time, buy recycled pencils or refillable pencils that can be used for years. There are even pencils out there made from rolled-up newspapers.

Art Project

Decoupage Project: Instead of throwing out a used shoe box or buying a new keep-safe holder, think decoupage. You should be able to find most of the supplies lying around the house. Decoupage works great on old picture frames too.

Box or frame
Cut-out pictures
Scissors
Glue
Popsicle stick
Lightly damp cotton cloth

1. Clean the surface of the item you plan to decoupage.

2. Cut out pictures from used magazines or catalogs. Be creative: You can even use printed poems or used coloring books.

3. Arrange the pictures before you add the glue so you know where you want everything. The pictures can be in any design and should overlap.

4. Completely coat the back of the picture with glue. You should also put a thin layer of glue on the area where you are sticking the picture.

5. Place the picture on the glue. Use your finger or the Popsicle stick to gently push down the picture (for a large picture, start from the center and work your way out) and push out any wrinkles and excess glue with the cloth.

6. Repeat the last two steps until all your pictures are glued on. Then let the glue dry completely.

7. Coat your entire item with diluted white glue (approximately three parts glue to one part water). Let this dry completely and enjoy.

WOW FACT!

One bus carries as many people as 40 cars. Ask your parents if you can take the bus instead of driving to school every day.

♫ When learning to play a new instrument that may be unavailable to rent—a piano for instance—ask your parents if you can purchase a used one or a new one that uses sustainable wood.

🎸 Old guitar strings can be used for funky bracelets or for hanging picture frames. And here's one better: If they're in reasonably good condition some strings can be donated to music-appreciation organizations that ship them to musicians in other countries.

★ Instead of buying new jewelry, ask your parents to clean out their closets and jewelry box to find pieces they don't wear anymore. You can have the old gold melted down and refashioned.

✄ Next time your favorite shampoo, body wash, or lotion bottle is empty, take it to a store that sells those items in bulk and refill your container. Many co-op and eco-minded grocery stores offer this option.

🖈 Look for "refill packs" when available for products such as baby wipes. They use up to 90 percent less packaging than regular, hard-plastic containers.

✳ Opt for soy- and veggie-based soaps (think shea butter and coconut oil) instead of conventional soaps, which are packed with petroleum-based chemicals and, especially if they're antibacterial, likely contain chemicals called parabens.

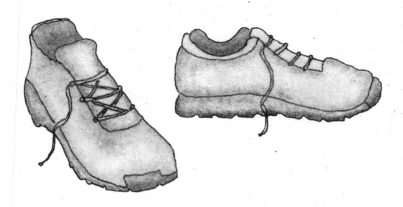

👟 Instead of tossing out your gently used running sneakers, find out where you can donate them to help people in need around the world. If your shoes have seen better days, they can still be recycled and turned into new sports surfaces at playgrounds and basketball courts.

💡 Seek out coloring books made from recycled paper. While you're at it, pick up some soy crayons to complete your eco-friendly art project.

🧺 Put recycling bins in every room of your home to encourage easy recycling of paper, plastics, and glass.

WOW FACT!

Americans throw away 28 billion glass bottles and jars every year. Instead of throwing them away, use them to store things like loose change, nuts and bolts, and crafting supplies.

☞ Instead of using toxic stain sticks, sprays, or bleaches, ask you mom or dad to pour boiling water on a new stain to make it disappear. (Sometimes club soda will do this trick, too.)

👓 Donate old prescriptive glasses or sunglasses to organizations that redistribute used frames to other areas of the world.

♪ Musical instruments come in such a variety of shapes, sizes, and materials that they are difficult if not impossible to recycle. However, some instruments may have metal parts that are recyclable or, at the very least, can be creatively reused. Think of selling, donating, or swapping your unused musical instruments when you are done with them.

✳ Choose a tube rather than a pump toothpaste. The hard plastic pump is not biodegradable and represents little more than fancy marketing and overpackaging.

✳ Use lemon juice or white vinegar for rinse after your shower. It will make your hair feel soft and shiny.

🏹 A new breed of umbrella is making its way in green circles. Look for the new ones that sport a bioplastic canopy and a lightweight, sustainable bamboo frame. The high-tech, heavy-metal-free plastic biodegrades when exposed to microbes in landfills, but not when it sits in your locker or closet. If all this sounds too futuristic for you, some innovative companies have developed umbrellas that use recycled detergent containers and toothpaste tubes instead.

➡ Ask your parents to return wire hangers to your wet-or drycleaner for recycling.

🥾 Rain-gear manufacturers are developing creative ways to repurpose materials (like plastic bottles), instead of making more PVC (polyvinyl chloride) plastic. When you need new rain boots or a new raincoat, first think if you can reuse ones from an older sibling or cousin. If that's not an option, perhaps you can investigate buying used rain gear. If not, look for gear that uses recycled plastic or polyester, or natural latex rubber.

🐦 With your parent's permission neatly cut up old pillowcases to make patches for your jeans. Used pillowcases can also be creatively made into laundry sacks by snaking a drawstring through the top.

Art Project

Go on an adventure and let your imagination run wild by making toilet-paper binoculars. Staple two toilet-paper rolls together side by side, then punch holes in the top sides of the rolls. Insert yarn through the holes and you have a strap to hang the binoculars around your neck. Personalize them with stickers and markers. If you want to add some color, use two rubber bands to attach colored cellophane on the end of each tube.

🦋 Two wire hangers twisted together make excellent butterfly or fairy wings for toddler dress-up games. Help a younger sibling to bend the hangers to a desired shape and then slide colorful hosiery over the oval-shaped "wings."

🌹 Old or outgrown kickboards can be used as kneepads in the garden.

◎ Not sure what to do with old stud earrings that you don't wear anymore? Repurpose them as bulletin board pushpins; brooches on sweaters, jacket lapels, and hats; or pushed into candles for fun decorations.

☺ Can there be anything more eco-friendly than a zero-emissions skateboard? Yes, a 100 percent sustainable skateboard. Look for the new breed of skateboard, which uses wood from sustainable forests, all-natural plant fibers, vegetable-based adhesives, and soy- or water-based paints.

🌲 When it's time to get a desk for doing homework, ask your parents to help you look for ones made from fallen trees instead of virgin wood.

Art Project

Bracelet Holder: Organize your jewelry and spare your recycling bin by making this bracelet holder.

Water-based paint
1 square block of wood
1 toilet-paper tube
Self-sticking shelf liner
Glue

1. Paint the wood block a bright color and decorate it as desired.

2. Cover the toilet-paper tube with self-sticking shelf liner and trim excess all around.

3. Glue the center of the tube perpendicular to the block so it looks like it's standing straight up like a rocket on its launchpad.

4. Let dry and then stack bracelets on tube.

✳ Brighten up your bathroom by buying a hemp shower curtain. They are naturally mildew resistant, can be easily machine washed, and far outlast ones made from vinyl.

♥ For carrying your homework and school supplies choose PVC-free backpacks. PVC (polyvinyl chloride) creates carcinogenic dioxins (the most potent cancer-causing agents known) in its manufacture, so instead choose stylish organic cotton and hemp knapsacks.

Reusing and recycling everyday products by making them into sustainable art is an inexpensive and fun way to help clean up the environment. Other forms of eco-art, such as using organic materials and botanicals, also serves as a creative way to embrace, honor, and showcase nature.

WOW FACT!

Each year Americans use about 600 pounds of paper per person. Printing on double-sided paper could reduce this number a lot.

If there's a baby brother or sister in the house advocate for all-natural, flushable, and biodegradable wipes. They're more eco-friendly than most as conventional baby wipes use fragrance, chlorine, synthetic preservatives, bleaching, and dioxin and take centuries to biodegrade. If it's not too much for your mom and dad you can even suggest that they make the switch to washcloths for cleaning baby. Likewise, cloth diapers should also be seriously looked at when a new baby joins the family.

✳ Instead of buying a new poster, create your own. Look through catalogs and magazines that are lying around your home. Cut out the pictures you like and use them as wall hangings, mini posters, locker decorations, and collages. The only supplies you need are a scissors, tape or glue, and your creativity and imagination.

If you're really bored on a rainy day or when you're traveling on vacation, make cereal box puzzles. Simply cut out fun and unusual shapes from one side of a cereal box, mix up the pieces, reassemble the puzzle, and repeat.

Art Project

CD Drink Coasters: Now that you're moving to downloadable music you might not know what to do with all your extra CDs. One word: coasters.

A few CDs
Scrap material, lace, cut-out photos
Glue
Felt

1. Use any old CDs.

2. Decoupage or glue scrap material on one side. If you use material, be sure that it's stretched and smoothed out with no bumps or creases. For a nice, seamless look, fold the material or decoupage photos over the edge and onto the bottom. Let dry.

3. Seal with diluted glue paste or decoupage glue. Let dry.

4 Cut out a circle of felt slightly smaller than the size of the CD.

5. Glue felt onto bottom and let dry.

Transform your empty mint tins into pretty barrette or bandage holders. Just clean, paint with water-based acrylic paints, and decorate with buttons, craft jewels, or ribbons. If you want to get fancy, glue magnets on the bottom and slap it on the inside of your locker as a mini first-aid box or sewing kit.

Not sure what to do with those photo booth strips you get at the arcade and zoo? Back them (using glue) with a thin cardboard strip the same size of the photo strip. Let dry and then punch a hole on the top. Slip a thin ribbon through and use as a bookmark.

Art Project

Sock Puppet: Recycle a sock and save a puppet. Here's a project that helps you find good use for the mates of all those socks that got lost in the laundry.

Cotton sock
Black marker
Sewing supplies or glue
Felt or scrap fabric
Scissors
Yarn
Loose buttons
Pipe cleaners (as desired)

1. Place hand in sock with thumb and fingers working like a mouth. (The sock should be large enough to fit loosely over your hand, covering your wrist bone.)

2. Mark the mouth, tongue, eyes, nose, hair, and ears with a black marker.

3. Cut ears and mouth from felt or scrap materials and sew or glue on marked areas. Eyes can be made from buttons.

4. Glue small strings of yarn to sock for hair (or mane, if you are making a horse).

5. Make antlers, horns, or antennas from pipe cleaners as desired.

CHAPTER 6
HEALTH AND FOOD

◔ Ask adults to take you to the nearest food market or grocery store. Make it fun by guessing where the food comes from (i.e., Washington State apples vs. Florida oranges vs. Brazilian bananas vs. Chilean sea bass). Think about all the travel and packaging that your food endures before it stands before you on the shelves and before it even hits your plate. Choose wisely and learn to recognize that healthy decisions can also be sound eco choices.

WOW FACT!

Twenty seven percent of all food produced each year in the United States for human consumption is tossed in the garbage. That amounts to 48 million tons of food wasted each year, or about 163 pounds of food by every person in this country. Approximately 49 million people could have been fed by that wasted food.

✗ Restrain yourself during meals and don't pile your plate with food you may not eat. You can always go back for seconds, but you can't save wasted food from being dumped in your trash and then a landfill.

✳ Fast-food establishments are one of the worst polluters of the environment, in the massive amounts of beef they raise, wasted packaging they produce, and energy that they use. And, for the most part, their food is tremendously unhealthy. When possible, avoid fast food and instead eat at home or at a sit-down restaurant. It's better for your digestion and for the environment. If you occasionally do hit the fast-food stops, choose your food wisely and opt for the salads and fruits and grilled foods.

✿ If you are able, have adults buy organic foods, which are grown without pesticides and chemical fertilizers. Not only does organic farming use 30 percent less energy than factory farms, but if you eat meat, organic animals are raised without antibiotics or artificial hormones and they aren't genetically modified (GM) or given GM feed. What a healthy option not only for you, but also for the planet!

☼ Search out organic sunblock and use it every day, even in winter. Do your research because not every sunscreen is created equal and some contain known allergens and carcinogens.

WOW FACT!

Approximately 500 chemicals are used in conventional farming compared to only four in organic farming. Try to eat organic whenever possible.

☉ When you are able, support local farming by visiting farmers' markets and co-ops. The fewer miles between the farm and your plate, the less energy must be expended on transportation, refrigeration, and packaging.

➡ Do your best to eat a diet rich in organic fruits and vegetables and less in meat. Raising animals for food requires massive amounts of land, food, energy, and water. In fact, the United Nations says that the meat industry generates more greenhouse gases than all the cars and trucks in the world combined and that it is "one of the most significant contributors to today's most serious environmental problems."

〰 Sea life around the globe is threatened by everything from pollution to overfishing. We are quickly running out of seafood and destroying the ecosystem in the process. Fish is good for you, and some species provide a great source of healthy Omega-3 fatty acids. Numerous organizations publish seafood guides. Choose your seafood carefully by buying sustainably harvested or farmed fish.

💲 Kick your winter cold with natural remedies like saline nose washes, and honey and hot lemon water instead of traditional medications. Natural concoctions are oftentimes better for your body and require fewer questionable chemicals to produce. They also cost less money for Mom and Dad.

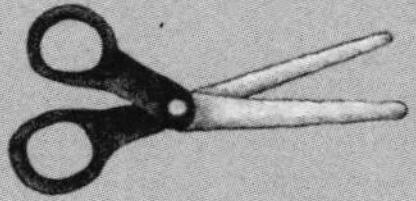

Art Project

Organic Play Dough: Instead of going to the store to buy play dough, be resourceful and use what you already have in your kitchen. Ask an adult to help you. Organic play dough is less expensive than store-bought brands and is better for the environment because there's no packaging, fragrances, or fuel consumption involved.

2 cups plain organic flour
1 cup salt
4 tablespoons cream of tartar
2 tablespoons organic oil
Natural food coloring
2 cups boiling water
Saucepan

1. Put all ingredients into a saucepan and cook on a low heat, stirring continuously.

2. When you get the right consistency of your play dough, take off the heat.

3. Wait until the dough is cool enough to knead. Knead until pliable. (For special occasion dough, add glitter before kneading stage.)

4. Store in an airtight container in the fridge. Will last up to a few months.

☺ Make the switch to paraben-free and all-natural cough drops and daily vitamins. Some drops and vitamins contain potentially toxic preservatives called parabens (a group of chemicals widely used as preservatives in the cosmetic and pharmaceutical industries) which can't be easily broken down by your body.

🏳 Don't smoke, ever. And if an adult in your life does smoke, ask him or her to stop for their sake, your sake, and the environment's sake. Not only is smoking bad for your body, but it's bad for our planet. The growing of tobacco involves deforestation and the use of large amounts of fertilizers, herbicides, and pesticides. Many of these are toxic and some contain known carcinogens. One cigarette butt alone, made of cellulose acetate tow (a plastic), can take ten years to degrade, and land and marine animals can die from eating harmful butts.

✳ Shine your leather shoes with natural alternatives like the inside of a banana peel or with olive oil, followed by a soft washcloth buff. Contact your local sanitation department to learn how to safely dispose of any old and toxic shoe polish.

➡ When it comes to freshening and clearing the air in your home, you should toss the artificial sprays, gels, and plug-ins. Not only is the packaging wasteful, but most products, even those labeled ALL NATURAL, contain dangerous chemicals such as benzene, formaldehyde, and phthalates that can aggravate asthma. For a green alternative, burn beeswax candles that are lightly scented without added chemicals. Or concoct a solution made from warm water and essential and citrus oils and keep it in a reusable spray bottle.

🏺 Ask your parents if you can help them replace conventional and mostly toxic household cleaners with more natural alternatives like olive oil for wood conditioning, distilled white vinegar and water for mirror and window cleaning, and baking soda for drain clogs and fridge fresheners. Borax, lemons, and club soda used in combination or by themselves also make great all-purpose cleaners. Making the switch reduces your family's exposure to toxic chemicals and saves energy that would have been used in the petroleum manufacturing process of making the products.

☺ When food shopping with your mom or dad check the PLU (price look up) code on the stickers stuck to your fruits and vegetables: a 4 at the beginning means conventionally grown produce, an 8 means the food has been genetically modified and a 9 means you've found organic.

🌿 Be creative about keeping moths out of your winter sweaters. Use a few drops of cedar wood oil or make own natural moth-repellent bags with dried rosemary, mint, thyme, ginseng, and whole cloves. They will keep the moths and carcinogenic naphthalene found in moth balls far away.

WOW FACT!

The average item purchased in your supermarket travels 1,400 miles by truck, train, or plane and driving a car just 20 miles releases about 22 pounds of CO_2. Try to eat locally grown produce to significantly reduce this figure.

✋ Most commercial hand sanitizers contain a large amount of alcohol, which makes them smell bad, can cause accidental alcohol poisoning, and can leave hands dry and cracked. Instead, look for all-natural wipes, sprays, or gels that kill 99.99 percent of germs with thyme oil and a combination of plant oils called ingenium. Of course, most of these brands are also not tested on animals.

☕ You may not be drinking much coffee yet, but that doesn't mean you don't know which type is better to buy. Encourage your parents to perk up in the morning with organic, fair-trade blends.

✳ That delicious buttery smell of microwave-popped popcorn is diacetyl, and it's not such a safe ingredient. Ditch the store-bought microwave popcorn with all its packaging and opt for a traditional air-popper or microwave your own concoction using a paper bag with organic kernels.

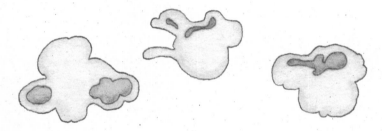

〰 Contrary to popular belief, fish, salt, and water cannot be labeled as organic because the USDA (United States Department of Agriculture) hasn't yet certified them. Let that knowledge guide the adults when deciding how much is fair to pay for seafood.

❗ Know how to read your food. A 100 PERCENT ORGANIC label means the product is entirely organic. An "organic" label means the product ingredients are at least 95 percent organic. A "made with/contains organic ingredients" means the ingredients are at least 70 percent organic. An "all natural" or "fresh" claim means absolutely nothing. And no, that's not a typo.

If you get a clogged drain, have your mom or dad use a metal plumber's "snake" or pour baking soda and white vinegar followed by boiling water down the drain.

➡ If your family needs a professional clean-up crew to put everything back in order after a big party, help them look for an eco-friendly cleaning company that has been awarded a Green Seal certification, an EcoLogo certification, or a Green Label by the Carpet and Rug Institute.

If your family's home is undergoing a paint job, make sure you're using organic clay paint. When looking beyond conventional paints you can easily find brands containing soy-based resins instead of petroleum-based acrylics. Most of these use no toxic materials like the VOCs (Volatile Organic Compounds) that most traditional paint companies use.

◎ When choosing glue for your art projects always reach for vegan eco-glue made without casein or any other animal derivatives. These nontoxic glues are usually water based and contain low VOCs and no hazardous air pollutants. Some even come in recyclable packaging.

☛ When picking out new pots and pans, tell your parents to skip the fancy nonstick ones. Teflon is made with a chemical, perfluorooctanoic acid (PFOA), that is a likely carcinogen and major polluter of air and water. Old-fashioned cast-iron pots and pans are a safe alternative, as are those made out of anodized aluminum and stainless steel (unless you're allergic to nickel).

To minimize health risks from cancer causing substances that can form when meats are grilled or broiled at high temperatures, ask your parents to choose lean organic meats and to trim the fat before cooking. Better still, have them grill more vegetables and fruits instead.

◎ For your papier-mâché projects at home or at school, use black-and-white newspaper strips and flour and water paste. Avoid instant papier-mâché kits, which may contain asbestos fibers and lead from pigments in colored printing inks.

🕯 Instead of discarding your small drinkable yogurt containers to the recycle bin, reuse them by making them into rattles for a baby brother or sister. All you need to do is wash and dry them, fill them ¹/₃ of the way with dry rice or beans, and seal the opening well with masking tape. They're the perfect size for little hands.

Art Project

Natural Dyes: Make natural dyes instead of using powdered tempera paints, pastels, chalks, or dry markers that release dust and decrease air quality. Making juice dyes is easy, but you'll need an adult's help.

½ cup plant material (walnut hulls, tea, canned beets, thawed frozen blueberries, etc.)
Water

1. Use the juice straight from thawed berries, or juice drained from canned beets.

2. Mix colors for hue variations. If using fresh berries, fruit, walnut hulls, or tea, combine the plant material with 1 cup of water in a pan and simmer over low heat for 30 minutes or so, adding more water as it evaporates.

🥾 A great alternative to a heating pad is making small, heated bean bags. Simply fill a clean sock with uncooked rice or beans and heat it up in the microwave. You can use them in bed, on the sofa while reading, or directly on your body to relieve an ache or pain.

💡 Slowly but surely start phasing out your chemical-ridden soaps and skin and hair products. Switching over to organic and biodegradable products is better for cleaning up your body and the groundwater. Start with products with heavy fragrances—these are the most likely to contain petroleum.

🏔 If you want to avoid animal-derived products, check your cosmetics labels for these ingredients: benzoic acid (which could be derived from certain birds, musk oxen, or elephants), carmine (from the cochineal beetle), cetyl alcohol (unless it specifies coconut or vegetable sources), glycerin (from animal fat), keratin (from horns, hooves, and feathers), lanolin (from sheep's wool), royal jelly (a bee secretion), silk powder (a silkworm secretion), stearic acid and urea (from animal urine and other fluids).

CHAPTER 7
SEASONS

🔥 Cozy up and save heating costs in winter by using your fireplace. Look for logs made of wood chips or sawdust, avoiding those that contain paraffin, a petroleum-based by-product. Some good alternatives include logs made of recycled cardboard boxes, recycled-paper briquettes, and logs made of used coffee grounds, which burn hotter and longer than wood while producing fewer emissions and less soot.

WOW FACT!

The amount of wood and paper we throw away each year is enough to heat 50 million homes for 20 years.

☀ In the summer, keep your curtains closed over sunny windows to reduce heat in your home. And in the winter, turn down the thermostat and leverage the sun's energy by pulling up shades and blinds to let the heat warm up your house.

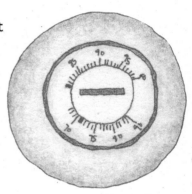

◐ Heating water is a big energy hog, especially in winter. A simple insulating blanket to improve the efficiency of your family's water heater costs only about $20 and is readily available at most hardware stores.

❗ Minimize the energy needed to heat your house or apartment by making sure your windows and doors are well sealed with caulking and weather stripping. This is a job for your parents, but tell them it can save as much as 10 percent of their winter heating costs.

$ Turning your thermostat down just 5 degrees in winter can cut energy bills and pollution by 10 percent, so try to keep it at 68 degrees Fahrenheit in winter, and 60 degrees or lower while you sleep. The cooler temperature will keep you awake for homework; and if you're chilly, you can always put on a sweater or add an extra blanket to your bed. It'll also keep the winter air moister and healthier.

✳ Ceiling fans aren't just for summertime. You can use your fan in the winter to keep your home warm without using as much heat. Run a ceiling fan clockwise, at a slow speed, to recirculate and push downward warmer air that accumulates at the ceiling. This can reduce energy consumption by up to 10 percent.

✳ After your adult has finished baking, turn off the oven and open its door to let the heat into your kitchen. You'll be amazed by how long the extra warmth lasts.

✳✳ When snow piles up in your driveway help your parents shovel instead of using gasoline-powered removal equipment. You'll use absolutely no energy but your own. Just be careful not to overdo it.

✳ Suggest to your parents that they not use rock salt in winter to defrost driveways and walkways, as salt speeds up corrosion of cars and bridges, ruins shoes, irritates pets' feet, chokes vegetation, and isn't very effective below 17 degrees Fahrenheit. Instead, help your family look for organic de-icers that won't cause a sticky mess like those that contain molasses, corn syrup, or beet juice.

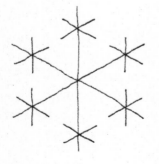

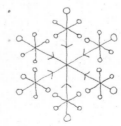

Art Project

All-Natural Cocoa Mint Lip Balm: Forget all the parabens and artificial flavors and colors. With adult supervision, make your own all-natural lip balm (adapted from the Museum of Science in Boston).

Saucepan
1 ½ tablespoons shea butter
1 tablespoon beeswax
1 ½ tablespoons cocoa butter
1 drop vitamin E
3–5 drops peppermint oil

1. Bring water to boil in a pan. Turn down to simmer.

2. Put shea butter, beeswax, and cocoa butter in a clean Pyrex jar and carefully set the jar in the pan of water.

3. Stir gently with a wooden spoon until the ingredients melt. Turn off stove.

4. Using a potholder, carefully remove jar from pan.

5. Add vitamin E and peppermint oil. (Both can be found in many health food stores, or you can ask an adult to order them online.) Stir well. Pour into clean containers.

6. Let cool and harden. Seal with a tight lid and label.

✿ Help out around the house and use a rake and your own energy instead of having your parents use a noisy, fuel-guzzling leaf blower.

🧹 Offer to broom-sweep the porch, stoop, or sidewalk in front of your house or apartment instead of having your mom or dad spray it down with a hose.

🍃 To keep warm in winter buy eco-fleece blankets that are made from recycled plastic beverage bottles.

◉ Instead of using plastic beach balls in summer, look for soft balls made from recycled sweaters. The eco-friendly stuffing is 100 percent recycled fiber and the balls are fun to kick around on both the grass and sand.

☀ To cool down in summer make iced tea and lemonade using organic sugar or agave, not artificial and possibly carcinogenic sweeteners.

CHAPTER 8
HOLIDAYS, CELEBRATIONS, AND BIRTHDAYS

Is your room overflowing with toys you don't use anymore? During the holiday giving season, ask yourself what you really need as opposed to what you really want. Also, encourage all the adults you know to think about the materials that your toys are made from and all the miles and packaging that your toys go through before they land nicely wrapped in gift paper at your home. Choose wisely and make a short list that takes into account the environmental impact your toys make.

WOW FACT!

Each year Americans dispose of more than 2.5 billion batteries, which end up in landfills leaking toxic mercury and cadmium. Using even just one rechargeable battery can replace anywhere between 50 and 300 disposables.

Have you ever felt disappointed after opening all your birthday gifts or holiday presents? Have you ever felt like it was just entirely too much stuff (too much quantity, not enough quality)? Ask yourself why our culture assumes it's so important to give and give and give. Think about your own resource consumption and ask the adults in your life to get you tickets to a ball game, movie, or concert instead.

Remember that shared experiences bring friends and family closer together, so give the gift of yourself by inviting someone to a play or by having a special meal together instead of wracking your brain for the perfect gift.

$ For your birthday, instead of accepting presents, invite your friends to donate money in your name to their favorite charity. Or, ask them to donate money to your favorite charity instead.

➡ For Father's Day chip in with other family members to get your dad or uncle a mulching lawnmower that spreads grass clippings back onto the lawn and decomposes and feeds the soil. If you have a small yard, manual reel mowers are a good green option, as are electric mowers that are quieter, cheaper, and save on fuel and pollution.

🎗 Spoil dad or grandpa on his birthday with an organic hemp necktie or new hemp messenger bag.

❗ For Father's Day encourage your dad and grandpa to use eclectic razors that can be solar-charged instead of disposed of. If they're set in their ways, buy them razors that have recycled handles made from old yogurt cups.

⌣ For Mother's Day look for pesticide-free bamboo, hemp, or organic cotton clothing instead of regular cotton. Exposing your mom to fewer pesticides is an even better gift.

Art Project

Paper Plate Maraca: After a picnic, start your own band using some clean paper plates.

2 dessert-sized paper plates
Stapler
Dried beans, rice, lentils, or small acorns
Magic markers
Stickers

1. Face two paper plates together. Staple around their rims, leaving a small hole.

2. Put beans, acorns, or rice in the hole and close it up using staples.

3. Decorate the bottoms of the plates with markers and stickers as desired.

Breakfast in bed, a homemade gift, and a big snuggle are better than any store-bought gift you can give your parents.

Buy mom or grandma vintage or recycled jewelry for Mother's Day. It has a history, but not a big carbon footprint.

With permission, buy iTunes online as a birthday gift for a friend or family member.

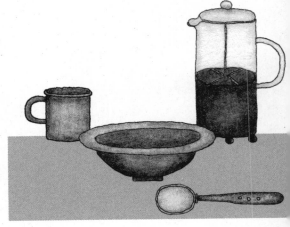

♥ Resist buying CDs and take the wrapping paper, plastic packaging, and drive to the store out of the picture while still giving the gift of music. Besides, the "jewel cases" that CDs come in are usually made from polyvinyl chloride, a dangerous compound that is difficult to recycle.

🎈 At birthday parties don't let balloons fly away. They can end up in a lake or ocean where a sea animal might choke on them. And make your choice latex instead of mylar. Mylar balloons take several hundred years to biodegrade in landfills while latex ones take about six months.

📋 Make homemade birthday cards and wrapping paper from newspaper, scrap fabrics, and artwork.

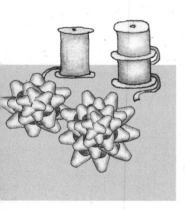

🎀 Reuse bows and tie packages with string, ribbon, or raffia that the recipient can reuse.

🎸 Ask your parents for music lessons, language classes, or a museum membership instead of more toys that you will likely lose interest in before your next birthday. An experience is usually more valuable than an object, anyway.

◎ Send electronic cards and invitations to save on paper and postage.

❗ Don't let your parents buy cheaply made plastic toys or individually wrapped trinkets for birthday favors. Instead, give away a personalized water bottle or a reusable knapsack or tote bag. Gifts like these are sure to be used for years instead of being thrown in the trash an hour after the party.

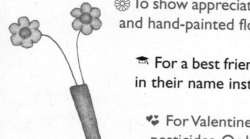

❀ To show appreciation for a favorite teacher give him or her a homemade and hand-painted flower pot with some extra-special seeds.

🎓 For a best friend's birthday or graduation, donate to a favorite charity in their name instead of buying him or her more stuff.

💕 For Valentine's Day buy organic flowers, which aren't treated with pesticides. Or better yet, buy a houseplant that will last for years, add oxygen to the air, and help reduce global warming.

✳ Buy organic and fair-trade chocolates for Valentine's, Easter, and Halloween.

🌐 Celebrate Earth Day in April by spreading the word about the importance of conservationism. Have your friends hand out flyers at school, write a letter to your local paper, or set up a community board meeting on local waste management.

⛳ If you have golf lovers in your family, introduce them to recycled tees. They're biodegradable and last longer than traditional wood tees, thus reducing tee box litter. Get some friends together on Arbor day and plant a tree!

🦃 A soy-based option, like tofurkey, is a good alternative for Thanksgiving. If not everyone in your family is ready to embrace the vegetarian way, choose an organic turkey or several organic chickens from a local farm. Incorporate seasonal vegetable side dishes like sweet potatoes, winter squash, and other root vegetables. After the feast, offer to help the adults clean and hand-dry the dishes.

🌲 Fake Christmas trees have high levels of lead, PVCs (polyvinyl chloride), and PCBs (polychlorinated biphenyl) that will stay in landfills for hundreds of years. If you don't have bad allergies, real trees are the more environmentally friendly choice. Don't worry about deforestation, 98 percent of American trees are farm-raised and they are usually replaced on a three-to-one basis after each harvest.

🌲🌲 Old Christmas trees should be composted or mulched to help create healthy new soil. Buy a tree with a root ball, then research to see if your city or town has a program to collect your potted tree and plant it in another neighborhood that needs more trees. Old Christmas trees make great winter habitats for rabbits.

☆ No matter what kind of tree you choose for Christmas, string it with energy-efficient LED lights.

🍃 Even greeting cards can be reused. Cut off the pretty fronts and use them as postcards. Or, recycle old holiday cards by turning the images into gift tags or new cards for next year.

★ For Hanukkah skip the electric menorah and do it the old fashioned way using soy or beeswax candles.

WOW FACT!

Recycled paper requires 64 percent less energy than making paper from virgin wood pulp, and can save many trees.

🐞 Ask for toys that are not battery operated or ones that only use rechargeable batteries. Batteries are not biodegradable and they're full of toxic heavy metals that can leak into landfills.

❗ Use reusable cotton shopping bags or pillowcases to carry your trick-or-treating candies.

💀 For your next Halloween costume, be creative and save cash by digging into the back of your closet or by visiting a thrift store to find clothes and accessories instead of buying new plastic costumes. Avoid masks made out of vinyl as latex ones are safer. Also, avoid fake, plastic jewelry as a lot of it contains lead.

➡ Buy an organic pumpkin from a local farm, make roasted pepitas from the seeds, and compost the jack-o-lantern when you're done.

Art Project

Are loose buttons burning a hole in your drawer? Glue orphaned buttons onto a bare flowerpot to spruce it up and put it on a windowsill or give as a gift.

WOW FACT!

On July 4th an estimated 60 million Americans fire up the barbecue grill. If your family is one of them, opt for a cleaner-burning propane or electric grill over one powered by charcoal, which contributes more to poor air quality. If you've got time to spare, a solar oven or stove avoids emissions altogether.

🌭 If your family does use charcoal, help them look for lump brands (briquettes may contain coal dust or other additives) made from invasive tree species or harvested from sustainably managed forests. Switch from lighter fluid, which releases smog-forming VOCs, to a chimney starter.

🍴 Set your picnic table with reusable dishware and cutlery and cloth napkins. If that doesn't work for your family, you can look for biodegradable or recycled-paper dinnerware, unbleached cups (not foam), and recycled-paper napkins.

🌸 Make your own organic sachet bags for holiday and birthday gifts using dried citrus peels, cinnamon, vanilla, dried flowers, or pine needles.

For any gadget-loving person in your life, buy a solar charger that can juice up a cell phone, MP3 player, digital camera, or portable game player. They even come in backpack or beach bag models.

If you're looking for a unique gift for older brothers or sisters in college, buy them a green city guide. Add to the theme and also get them a green coupon book with discounts and free offers at environmentally friendly businesses in their new home city.

Look for snow- and surfboards that use Forest Stewardship Council (FSC)—certified wood products without compromising style and performance. Also look for boards that have their top sheets silk-screened with water-based or soy ink, thereby reducing plastics and solvents. Light, fast, and durable bamboo boards are easier on the environment than conventional VOC-emitting fiberglass and polyurethane and durable epoxy boards use a resin that emits $2/3$ less VOCs than polyester resins.

If you are lucky enough to be in a wedding party as the ring bearer or flower girl, ask the bride and groom to have their guests throw birdseed as they exit the church. It's an eco-friendly and smart way to start off the marriage, because there will be less waste (unlike plastic bottles of bubbles) and it won't make some birds sick (unlike rice).

As a birthday present for a sports fan consider buying a football, volleyball, or soccer ball from a company that manufactures equipment from eco-certified materials. That means the rubber comes from FSC—certified trees and the outer cover is vegan. Some forward-thinking sports equipment companies even use unions and employ rigorous labor standards.

After a birthday party, turn all those liter-size plastic bottles hanging around into doorstops. Remove the label and thoroughly clean and dry each bottle. Fill all the way with sand or dirt. Close using original top. Decorate using water-based paints or decoupage.

Art Project

Snow Globe: Turn baby food jars into magical wonderlands in a few easy steps. These make great gifts!

Small baby food or other glass jar with lid
Baby oil or corn syrup
Water
Glitter
Glue
Small toy or seashell (optional)

1. Fill the jar with baby oil or corn syrup, and a little water.

2. Add glitter.

3. Glue a toy or seashell to the lid and let dry.

4. Put the lid on the jar and seal with waterproof glue.

5. When dry, turn the jar upside down and shake. (When in regular position the globe will be standing on the jar's lid.)

CHAPTER 9

AWARENESS AND ACTION

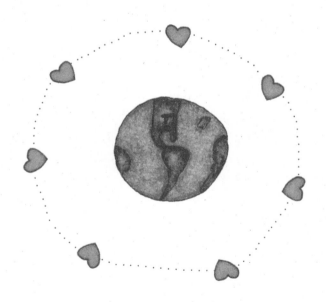

☞ Educate yourself about environmental injustice (the unfair distribution of ecological damage). For instance, have you ever wondered why pollution-filled transportation projects or landfill sites disproportionately impact minority and low-income populations?

WOW FACT!

In the United States the single most important factor in predicting the location of hazardous-waste sites is the ethnic composition of a neighborhood. Three of the five largest commercial hazardous-waste landfills in America are in predominantly black or Hispanic neighborhoods.

❗ Read up and learn how you can become an advocate for environmental justice (the right to a safe, healthy, productive, and sustainable environment for all, fair treatment and meaningful involvement of all people regardless of race, color, national origin, or income). Talk to local environmental groups and politicians to learn how to identify and address the effects of transportation projects on the public, especially adverse impacts to minority or low-income populations and then inquire as to what you and your friends can do about it.

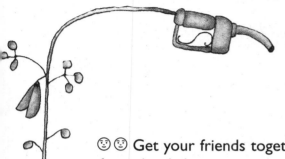

Get unplugged at least one day per week. It's not necessary to be accessible 7 days per week and 24 hours per day. Pick a day that you can stop texting, IMing, and e-mailing so you can spend valuable face time with your siblings, parents, grandparents, cousins, and close friends without being annoyingly distracted and distant.

Do your research on fuel consumption, greenhouse emissions, wasting food and trash, energy consumption, and preserving habitats and help educate your friends, younger siblings, and even your parents and grandparents.

Get your friends together to form an eco-club or after school clean-up crew.

Plan a green movie night at your home and feature a documentary about global warming or the environment. If you want to go all out, serve organic snacks and give away hemp tote bags and reusable water bottles.

Take a walk in your neighborhood and choose the oldest looking tree you can find. Guess how old it is and think about all it has "seen and done" in its lifetime. At the very least, it's provided shelter, helped clean the air, and hosted people's picnics.

➡ Do some research and identify an "environmental hero." Someone like Rachel Carson, Majora Carter, Alison Gannett, Annie Leonard, Wangari Maathai, or John Muir. Write an extra-credit book report on that person.

✦ Get inspired by nature. Take a walk though the woods, lay on your tummy and watch the ants go by, wonder at the small things that make the planet work the way it does.

🚀 Interview a grandparent or an older person to find out what it was like to grow up without some of the technology that we have today. How do you think the technology we have now—electricity, cars, computers, phones, plastics, ocean and space research—impacts the planet? Think about both the positive and negative effects.

🌐 Learn how to protect the planet by reading books and subscribing to daily online green tips by both local and national environmental organizations.

WOW FACT!

It takes 90 percent less energy to recycle aluminum cans than to make new ones. Encourage all of your friends to recycle their used soda cans.

🔗 Volunteer your time to help out at a local eco-friendly business or environmental nonprofit.

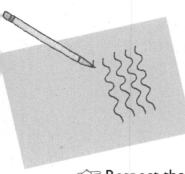

🖊 Make your voice heard by writing letters to your local paper praising businesses who embrace green practices and products.

💲 Donate some of your allowance or birthday money to green causes that capture your interest.

☞ Respect the environment and treat it like you would your own body.

WOW FACT!

According to the EPA (Environmental Protection Agency), up to 80 percent of Americans' trash can be recycled, but only 25 percent actually is.

➡ We each see more advertisements in one year than people 50 years ago saw in a lifetime. Use the tips here to distinguish environmentally safe products from those that are just falsely advertised.

🐦 Everything that is labeled NATURAL and ORGANIC is not necessarily sustainable and animal friendly. Some companies try to appear more environmentally friendly than they actually are—it's called greenwashing. Reading up on consumer goods companies and ingredient labels can help you avoid buying into false claims.

➡ Become a community activist. Increase your circle of influence at home and at school and find out how you can improve your town's or city's waste reduction and recycling programs.

🌐 Talk to your parents about supporting political candidates that have a sustainable environmental agenda.

❗ Take a pledge of responsibility for taking care of and healing our planet.

☺☺ The greatest thing you can do to save the planet is to inspire someone else to care as deeply as you already do. Be sure to talk about what you're doing to protect wild places, conserve energy, and keep our air and water clean. Talking about the issues you've learned about in this book helps raise awareness, builds community, and can inspire others to action.

☞ Conduct an audit and give your school or your home a green report card. Evaluate how school administrators or your parents are doing and make helpful recommendations on where they can improve.

WOW FACT!

• •

The United States makes up 5 percent of the world's population, but we're consuming 30 percent of the world's resources and creating 30 percent of the world's waste. Consume less!

INDEX